Series consultant: Dr Terry Jennings

Designed by Jane Tassie

The author and publishers would like to thank Ire, Chelsey
and the staff and pupils of the Charles Dickens J & I School, London,
for their help in making this book. Thanks also to Gaston Saint-Pierre,
Phil Pickford, and Edward and Barbara Gould.

A CIP record for this book is available from the British Library.

ISBN 0-7136-6326-X

First paperback edition published 2002
First published 1999 in hardback by A & C Black Publishers Limited
37 Soho Square, London WID 3QZ
www.acblack.com

Text copyright
© 1999 Nicola Edwards and Jane Harris
Photographs copyright
© 1999 Julian Cornish-Trestrail

Typeset in 23/28pt Gill Sans Infant and 25/27 pt Soupbone Regular

Printed in Singapore by Tien Wah Press (Pte.) Ltd

A & C Black uses paper produced with elemental chlorine-free pulp,
harvested from managed sustainable forests.

Science Explorers

Wool

Exploring the science
of everyday materials

Nicola Edwards and
Jane Harris

Photographs by
Julian Cornish-Trestrail

A & C Black · London

Look at
these things
we've collected.

They
are all made
from wool.

2

3

Most wool comes from sheep.
It's the sheep's springy coat.

This is raw wool. It's a bit greasy.

Sheep are shorn once a year. Their wool coats are washed and dried, then combed to remove the tangles.

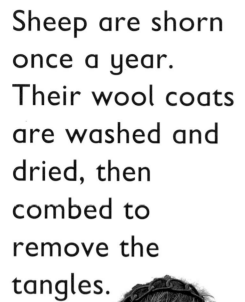

Don't worry, it doesn't hurt!

This wool has been dyed blue.
A machine is twisting it into
long pieces of thread.

Look at all these balls of wool. They have been dyed different colours and some threads are thicker than others.

I'm choosing a light-coloured ball.

I'm choosing a dark-coloured ball.

8

Wool is woven
into clothes
in factories.

You can also knit
your own clothes
with knitting
needles.

I'm helping my mum
to knit a scarf!

I feel cold, so I'm putting on a woollen jumper.

It feels a bit rough on my skin.

My scarf is softer than the jumper.

It feels warm and smooth.

11

Let's try pulling the raw wool. It's stretchy, too. It's also quite strong.

I have to pull hard to pull it apart.

14

Woollen clothes keep us warm.
The tiny hairs in the wool
help stop the heat
escaping from
our bodies.

I feel really snug and warm.

We've just been outside in the rain. My woollen jumper feels damp on the outside but I'm still dry underneath.

Damp wool smells a bit funny.

My T-shirt is not made from wool. The rain has soaked through.

Yuk! I feel cold and wet.

I'm washing my woollen gloves carefully. If the water is too hot, my gloves will shrink!

The wool soaks up the water.

The gloves feel heavy.

My gloves
are clean and
dry now.

They're
much lighter.

19

Felt is made of wool that has been rolled and pressed together to make it flat.

This piece of felt has been burnt, but it didn't catch fire.

I can see the burnt hairs through the magnifying glass.

Firefighters' uniforms used to contain a special felt.

The felt helped protect firefighters from the flames.

What shall we do with these old jumpers? The wool is still as good as new.

23

Notes for parents and teachers

The aim of the *Science Explorers* series is to introduce children to ways of observing and classifying materials, so that they can discover the various properties which make them suitable for a range of uses. By talking about what they already know about materials from their everyday use of different objects, the children will gain confidence in making predictions about how a material will behave in different circumstances. Through their explorations, the children will be able to try out their ideas in a fair test.

pp 2–3

Wool was first used for clothing thousands of years ago. In 4,000 BC people began to make cloth from wool by matting the wool together and spinning it into thread. The Romans made togas out of fine wool. By the beginning of the fourteenth century, wool was an important source of wealth in Britain.

Wool is chiefly used to make clothing, but ask the children to look for other things that can be made of wool, for example, carpets, paint rollers, slippers, tennis balls and curtains.

pp 4–5

Wool is a fibre that comes from the fleece of sheep and other animals including goats (mohair and cashmere), rabbits (angora) and llama (alpaca). The fibres grow like hair from roots in the skin and have a natural waviness or crimp. The hairs are covered with tiny scales and with a natural greasy coating, called lanolin. Show the children a picture of a magnified wool fibre so that they can see the scaly coating. Make sure the children always wear protective gloves when handling raw wool.

pp 6–7

A sheep's coat, the fleece, is shorn in spring or summer. The fleeces are washed to remove seeds, mud, dung and lanolin. Then the wool is dried and fed through a carding machine, which combs the wool so that all the fibres are pointing in the same direction. This turns the wool into a flat mat which is cut into narrow strips. Spinning machines twist the strips into yarn. The children could try carding some wool using a comb or a hairbrush.

pp 8–9

Wool is highly absorbent, making it easy to dye. Usually it is dyed before being knitted or woven. Yarn can be knitted and woven by hand or by machine. The children could try out some simple knitting or weaving.

pp 10–14

The type and quality of wool can make it feel very different – some wool feels soft and smooth against the skin, while other types feel itchy and scratchy. The children could compare garments made from different types of wool, for example, a lambswool sweater and an Arran sweater. Wool is stretchy and springy because of its natural crimp.

p 15

Pockets of air trapped between the wool fibres stop the heat escaping from our bodies. By looking at a knitted garment through a magnifying glass, the children will be able to see the individual fibres, helping them to understand how wool insulates.

pp 16–19

Give the children a selection of woollen clothes and other garments made from artificial fibres. See if they can work out which are made from wool and which are not. Do the clothes feel and smell different? The children could test them for stretchiness, strength and absorbency. Wool is water resistant and will hold a lot of moisture before feeling damp, which is why wool coats help sheep to stay dry in the rain. Wool needs to be washed with care because the overlapping scales can cause wool to shrink and mat together if washed in hot soapy water.

pp 20–21

Felt is matted wool. Until the early 1990s, wool was used in firefighters' uniforms because it does not continue to burn when removed from a flame. Can the children think of any other people who would need to wear similar protective clothing for their work?

pp 22–23

Wool is very durable and hard-wearing. Today there are many artificial alternatives to wool, including acrylic, nylon and polyester. Sometimes these are blended with wool. Artificial fibres are cheaper to make, but they lack many of wool's special qualities. The children could look at the labels of a selection of clothes and make a list of the different materials.

Find the page

Here are some of the words and ideas in this book.

colouring pen 3

damp wool 16

describing wool 4, 5, 10, 11, 12, 13, 14

felt 20, 21

firefighters' uniforms 21

knitting 9, 23

recycling wool 23

rough wool 10

sheep 4, 5, 6

soft wool 11

stretching wool 12, 13, 14

washing wool 18, 19

woollen clothes 9, 10, 11, 12, 13, 15, 16, 22, 23